THE NEW YORK WORLD'S FAIR
1939/1940

THE NEW YORK WORLD'S FAIR

1939/1940 in 155 photographs

by Richard Wurts and Others

Selection, Arrangement and Text by STANLEY APPELBAUM

DOVER PUBLICATIONS, INC., NEW YORK

Frontispiece: The Administration Building and the 1939 World's Fair flag. The facade sculpture *Mithrana* by Albert Stewart represented the Spirit of the Fair unveiling the future. This photo by Richard Wurts was used on the title page of the *Official Guide Book of the New York World's Fair 1939.*

Published in Canada by General Publishing Company, Ltd., 30 Lesmill Road, Don Mills, Toronto, Ontario.
Published in the United Kingdom by Constable and Company, Ltd., 10 Orange Street, London WC2H 7EG.

The New York World's Fair 1939/1940 is a new work, first published by Dover Publications, Inc., in 1977.

International Standard Book Number: 0-486-23494-0
Library of Congress Catalog Card Number: 77-70029

Manufactured in the United States of America
Dover Publications, Inc.
180 Varick Street
New York, N.Y. 10014

ACKNOWLEDGMENTS

Editor and publisher owe the greatest debt of thanks to the lenders of the photographs, without whose cooperation this publication would not have been possible. (The numbers are those of the illustrations in this book.)

Richard Wurts lent the following Wurts Bros. photos: 2–5, 8–16, 22, 23, 26–28, 31, 32, 34, 36, 37, 39–44, 46, 47, 49–57, 63, 69, 71–73, 76–78, 80, 81, 85–89, 91–95, 98–101, 103, 105–107, 109–111, 113, 114, 116, 118–120, 123–125, 129–132, 142–145, 150, as well as the frontispiece and the three illustrations in the Introduction.

The General Electric Company furnished the photo (58) of the Rockwell Kent mural, and kindly gave permission to reproduce it.

John F. H. Gorton, Director of The Rockwell Kent Legacies, lent the original squared-off print of Kent's cartoon for the mural (59), and kindly gave permission to reproduce it.

The General Motors Corporation kindly consented to the reproduction of two photos (20 and 21) from their 1940 booklet *Futurama*, issued at the Fair.

All the other photographs were lent by the Museum of the City of New York, through the courtesy of Joseph Veach Noble, Director, and A. K. Baragwanath, Senior Curator. Among the Museum's prints, the following bore credits to photographers:

Sigurd Fischer: 75, 150.

Samuel H. Gottscho: 18, 25, 30, 67, 68, 115, 138, 147 (the last four given as Gottscho-Schleisner).

Michael L. Radoslovich: 84.

Underwood & Underwood: 74, 122.

Carl Van Vechten: 6, 7, 35, 65, 96, 97, 102, 117, 126–128, 133–135, 137, 139–141, 146, 148, 149, 151. The photos by this famous writer are technically inferior to the others in the book, but are invaluable for their attention to details of sculpture and amusement exhibits not otherwise documented in the sources available to us.

Westinghouse Electric and Manufacturing Company: 60.

In addition, thanks are due to Miles Kreuger, President of the Institute of the American Musical, Inc., who permitted me to consult his important collection of World's Fair memorabilia.

And love to my sister Faye, with whom I saw the Fair.

New York   STANLEY APPELBAUM
August 25, 1976

GREAT WHITE WAY

EXHIBITS

THE WORLD'S FAIR IN 1940

Several buildings and areas had had different designations in 1939. The changes in the Great White Way (1939: Amusement Area) along Liberty Lake (1939: Fountain Lake), and those in the Court of States, were too numerous to indicate here. The chief alterations in the principal Zones, marked on this map by asterisks, were:

1940		1939
America at Home	=	Home Furnishings
American Art Today	=	Contemporary Art
American Common	=	U.S.S.R.
American Legion	=	Georgia (state)
American Standard	=	American Radiator & Standard
Coca-Cola	=	Food Bldg. South (No. 3)
FWA	=	WPA
Hall of Industry	=	Metals
L1 (Operations)	=	Hall of Special Events
Maritime Transport & Communications	=	Communications
Power	=	Electrical Products
White Owl	=	General Cigar Co.
World of Fashion	=	Consumers
Z1 (Operations)	=	Marine Transportation
(unidentified bldg. in Food Zone)	=	Distilled Spirits
(unidentified bldg. in Government Zone)	=	Netherlands
(unidentified bldg. in Production Zone)	=	Operations Bldg. of Zone

INTRODUCTION

Chicago had dazzled the world with its Columbian Exposition of 1893—the source of the Ferris wheel and the consecration of Beaux Arts architecture in America—and had scored high with its Century of Progress fair in 1933/1934. Philadelphia had hallowed its past at the 1876 Centennial—which featured the telephone—although its 1926 Sesqui-Centennial was a failure. The Louisiana Purchase Exposition (St. Louis, 1904) and the Panama-Pacific Exposition (San Francisco, 1915) were bewitching, and many a smaller American city, not to mention world capitals like Paris, had put on successful shows.

Yet New York City, financial center of the nation, and its reputed cultural center as well, had housed no fairs since 1853, when it had responded in a low key to the first great international industrial fair of modern times, Prince Albert's Crystal Palace exposition in London, 1851. But when the sleeping giant was roused, it produced a spectacle that no one who was there has forgotten, and that remains a touchstone for future exhibitors.

The Depression of the 1930s was not yet shaken off, and business needed a stimulant, when in May 1935 a Jackson Heights engineer, Joseph F. Shagden, and a distant relative of the President, Edward F. Roosevelt, presented the idea of the Fair to an appreciative group of New York businessmen. A steering committee began meetings in June and by October a nonprofit corporation for educational purposes (profits to go to city and state charities) had been formed. After a temporary bank loan, the Fair Corporation sold about 27 million dollars' worth of bonds (at four percent, payable in 1941) to businesses, unions and the public, and received sizable private contributions from local millionaires.

Although the Flushing, Queens, locale chosen for the Fair was the geographical and population center of the city, it was still most unusual: the activities of the Long Island Rail Road, in conjunction with the indifference of contractors and politicians, had turned the marshy area into a garbage dump of monumental proportions, characterized by F. Scott Fitzgerald in his 1925 novel *The Great Gatsby* as "a valley of ashes—a fantastic farm where ashes grow like wheat into ridges and hills and grotesque gardens . . . bounded on one side by a small foul river" (the Flushing River).

The clearance of this site for the Fair was the largest land reclamation project in the eastern United States. (Grand Central Parkway, connecting the Triborough Bridge to eastern Long Island, had already cut through the dump in 1932.) Park planning began in January 1936, the groundbreaking ceremonies were held on June 29, 1936, and the land was graded by March 1937. Another remarkable aspect of the enterprise was that, for the first time in history, firm arrangements had been made to turn over the exposition grounds to the local government after the Fair for a municipal park. Through thick and thin, energetic New York City Parks Commissioner Robert Moses (later to be president of the 1964/1965 fair at the same location) never lost sight of his own goal: Flushing Meadows Park.

Eventually the city spent about 26.7 million dollars for reclamation and its permanent Fair building. New York State, which offered its own temporary building and the permanent amphitheater that housed the *Aquacade*, spent about $6.2 million; the federal government, some three million. Foreign nations paid between 30 and 35 million for their pavilions. The Fair Corporation's

The photographer Richard Wurts, who took 93 of the pictures in this book, as he looked in 1938. He is holding a print of the photo reproduced facing the title page. He was then at work on his one-man show *Building the 1939 New York World's Fair*, held at the Museum of the City of New York from November 2, 1938, to January 9, 1939.

construction outlay was about 42 million, and 52 million came from other sources (exhibitors, concessionaires and so on). Total investment: about 160 million dollars. It was decided that 40 percent of daily receipts (as well as rentals, etc.) would go toward paying off the Corporation's bonds; the first two million dollars of net revenue was to be given to the city outright for the final work in preparing the park after the Fair; the next 1.7 million would also go to the city, for extending the Independent subway system up to the Fair grounds; then any net revenue remaining would be for local charities.

It was hoped that visitors to the Fair would set about a billion dollars flowing through New York City, and that the City would lose some of its bad reputation for aloofness and remoteness from the rest of the country. When it appeared that it would be possible to open in the spring of 1939, a patriotic pretext was hit upon for the Fair: opening day, April 30, would be the 150th anniversary of Washington's inauguration as President at Federal Hall in New York City. A huge statue of the Father of His Country was commissioned from the revered sculptor James Earle Fraser, and Washington's name and face appeared here and there at the exposition. But the only real George Washington memorabilia were relegated to a modest and remote pavilion in the Amusement Area, the Sons of the American Revolution Building. And there was no chance of being misled as to the purpose of the Fair if you scanned the roster of the Corporation.

The Executive Committee of the Board of Directors consisted of: Winthrop W. Aldrich (chairman of the board of Chase Manhattan Bank), Mortimer N. Buckner (chairman of the board of the New York Trust Company), Floyd L. Carlisle (chairman of the board of the Consolidated Edison Company), John J. Dunnigan (majority leader of the New York State Senate), Harvey Dow Gib-

son (president and chairman of the board of Manufacturers Trust Company), Mayor Fiorello La Guardia, George McAneny (chairman of the board of the Title Guarantee and Trust Bank), Thomas H. McInnerney (president of the National Dairy Products Corporation), Bayard F. Pope (chairman of the board of the Marine Midland Corporation), Percy S. Straus (president of Macy's), Frank J. Taylor (the City Comptroller), Matthew Woll (the third vice-president of the American Federation of Labor) and—easily the most fascinating personality directly associated with the Fair, and its president both years—Grover Aloysius Whalen.

At this time Whalen was chairman of the board of the Schenley Products Company, but he had a long record in the field of merchandising and business consultation, having been associated with Coty Perfumes (which had a prominently situated pavilion at the Fair), John Wanamaker and the IRT subway system, to name just a few firms. As far back as 1919 he was already known as a gracious welcomer of official visitors to New York City, and it was he who arranged the tumultuous reception for Lindbergh in 1927. From the end of 1928 to the middle of 1930 he was the City's Police Commissioner; in the latter year he became notorious for his violent disruptions of left-wing gatherings. As local head of the National Recovery Administration in the early days of the New Deal, he settled some 130 labor disputes. A man of infinite tact, charm and connections, he was invaluable to the Fair both as a figurehead and as an indefatigable worker and organizer.

One of Whalen's most remarkable contributions was in rounding up foreign exhibitors in a period of financial stress and gathering war clouds. President Roosevelt had issued a hearty invitation, and in 1937 the Bureau International des Expositions in Paris had decreed that the New York Fair would be *the* 1939 exposition endorsed for participation by its signatory nations, but there was still tough practical resistance to be overcome during Whalen's European trip. Curiously enough, the Soviet Union was the first foreign country to comply (and this despite Whalen's anti-red record!), and allotted four million dollars for its pavilion, which a Gallup poll later showed to be the most popular in the foreign area. Western Europe, thus challenged, could not lag behind. Altogether, a record 60 nations and international organizations took part in the Fair. Germany was conspicuous by its absence, no doubt because it was saving its money for the war—although it was also reported that Hitler would never exhibit in a city whose mayor had called his country "a museum of horrors."

It was also remarkable that 33 states of the Union and territories responded favorably to the invitation of Governor Herbert E. Lehman. All this cooperation enabled the Fair Corporation to dwell on another of their goals: to demonstrate the interdependence of all states and countries in the twentieth-century world.

But if businessmen, diplomats and patriots had created the basis for the Fair, it was a different group of men, a new breed of the Thirties, who gave it its physical aspect, a great deal of its spirit and its abiding theme: "Building the World of Tomorrow." These were the industrial designers, men like Norman Bel Geddes, Raymond Loewy, Henry Dreyfuss and Walter Dorwin Teague, who, coming from careers in theatrical design or other artistic backgrounds, had persuaded the large American corporations that beauty—of the Bauhaus and Art Deco persuasion—could sell their products. Fashioning hundreds of commodities from toothbrushes to ocean liners in clean, uncluttered lines and surfaces, they had added the word "streamlined" to the consciousness of the country.

The Fair might well have been a stodgy curio show had the industrial designers not won the day little by little, assisted by architects, painters and sculptors who had already made a mark in civic projects of the Thirties such as Rockefeller Center or who had grown to artistic maturity under the auspices of the federal projects of that decade. Fortunately, not only did the Fair Corporation heed the suggestions of these leading designers, not only did these men work on the pavilions of many private companies, but, what is more, the Board of Design of the Fair, established in the spring of 1936, was imbued with their principles and drew up rules and guidelines that helped immeasurably to make the exposition perspicuous in organization and tasteful in execution.

With the spires of Manhattan visible in the distance it was felt desirable to give the Fair a low silhouette, broken here and there by towers and pylons, and, of course, by the Trylon, the highest structure on the grounds. The pavilions were to be outspoken exhibition architecture, imaginative but not alarming (unfavorable public reaction to "excesses" of 1933 Chicago fair buildings was vividly recollected). Replicas of historical buildings and extremely traditional structures were outlawed, except in the Government Zone (especially the Court of States) and the Amusement Area. Since windows would eat up exhibition wall space and would make the buildings too hot in the middle of the summer, air conditioning was generally used and most of the pavilion exteriors had extensive unbroken surfaces, relieved by murals or relief sculpture. Signs were not allowed to protrude.

The Fair Corporation Board of Design conceived and constructed a number of buildings at an early stage to show the way—chiefly its own administration and operations buildings as well as those that were to house the focal exhibits of the various zones (these focal buildings also had a multiplicity of small exhibitors), but also a few for large private exhibitors. The Board of Design buildings were characterized by steel frames and curtain walls of gypsum board, wire lath and stucco. Many of the private architects followed suit, but there were also interesting variations. For instance, asbestos boards were used on the AT&T building, redwood on the Contemporary Art Building, a stainless-steel shell for the U.S. Steel Building, and so on. In many cases native materials or products (marble, tile) were used on foreign and state buildings. The constructions of the Design Board and of the private American corporations were often as much pieces of sculpture as of architecture, and though usually "abstract," would sometimes be partially or wholly representational or emblematic, as with RCA's radio-tube shape or the twin prows of the Marine Transportation Building. All in all, there were about 375 structures of all types at the Fair, including 100 major exhibit buildings (about a third done by the Board of Design) and 50 major amusement concessions.

Sound was also regulated, no outside spiels being countenanced unless deemed essential to the show.

The regulation of color, as far as it went, was of great interest. At the 1933 Chicago fair, the famous designer Josef Urban had been a sort of color czar, given wide powers to oversee the effects. In New York, the Board of Design laid down topographical prescriptions to exhibitors in a large central area of the Fair. The Trylon and Perisphere were to be dead white, the immediately surrounding area (Theme Center) off-white. The main axis of the Fair (Constitution Mall) was conceived in reds, growing deeper—from rose to burgundy—with remoteness (in a northeasterly direction) from the Theme Center. The Avenue of Patriots, veering off to the north from the Theme Center, would have basically yellow pavilions, ending in deep gold; the Avenue of Pioneers, heading east, would have blue, ending in deep ultramarine. The curved thoroughfare that connected the three ends

was called Rainbow Avenue and had appropriately shifting colors. Naturally, slight variations as well as murals and sculptures relieved any possible monotony, but there were also many subtle tricks played with complementary colors and other relationships.

Night lighting was also carefully planned. Floodlighting was allowed only on the Perisphere and a very few other spots. A searchlight canopy (the searchlight had been one of the thrills at Chicago in 1893!) played over the Court of Peace near the Federal Building. Otherwise (not counting fireworks and special light shows over the two main sheets of water) only relatively restrained—though bright, colorful and inventive—illumination was allowed. One of the triumphs of the Fair was the new white fluorescent street lighting, but in addition many special effects (such as partially buried high-intensity mercury capillary lamps under rows of trees that made the leaves glow green) were heartily applauded.

Many of the suggestions, both stylistic and practical, for illumination and light fixtures came from the 1937 Paris exposition (Arts et Techniques), which was visited by New York Fair personnel. Other Parisian ideas that were influential in Flushing Meadows affected the nightly *son et lumière* shows, the various means of transportation within the Fair grounds, the use of exterior murals and the general tone of the profusely scattered relief and free-standing sculptures and applied ornament in the Moderne, or Art Deco, style. Even the layout of the main geographical axis of the New York Fair—from the Theme Center to the Federal Building—may have been inspired by the 1937 French example.

But an absolutely new feature of the 1939 Fair was called for by its almost unprecedented magnitude (it covered 1216½ acres, extending about 3½ miles south from Flushing Bay, with a maximum width of 1¼ miles; only the 1904 St. Louis fair was slightly greater in area). This feature was the system of zoning by exhibit categories. The seven geographical zones were [my numbering] (1) Communications and Business Systems and (2) Production and Distribution (these two flanked the Theme Center fairly symmetrically), (3) Community Interests and (4) Food (these balanced each other a little farther away from the Theme Center), (5) Government (grouped around the Lagoon of Nations at the end farthest from the Theme Center), (6) Transportation (across the Grand Central Parkway from the Theme Center) and (7) the Amusement Area (grouped around the lake, and across World's Fair Boulevard—later Horace Harding Boulevard, now the Long Island Expressway—from the main part of the grounds). All of these but Government and Amusement had a "focal exhibit," a noncommercial display prepared and run by the Fair Corporation, in one building within the zone. There were also two exhibit categories, (8) Medicine and Public Health and (9) Science and Education, that were practically all focal exhibit with no geographical extension; they were housed in one building complex inside the Community Interests Zone. This zoning was strictly adhered to, although as things turned out, and for different reasons, New York City, New York State, Florida, Sweden and Turkey were located outside the Government Zone.

The lagoon and the lake had been created on those marshy areas that would have been hardest to fill. The highest ground in the Fair area was where the Theme Center, the New York City Building and Ford and General Motors were located.

The Fair opened on schedule on April 30, 1939; the paying customers on that day numbered 198,791. General admission was 75 cents for adults (rather high in the days when the subway ride to the Fair cost a nickel) and 25 cents for children

from three to 14. Season tickets and other special arrangements were offered. There were separate admission charges to a number of exhibits and concessions, comprising possibly a fourth of the Fair; it was estimated that a visitor who went to all of these would have to pay a total of $14.15. The grounds opened daily at 9 A.M., the exhibit buildings remaining open until 10 P.M., the Amusement Area until 2 A.M. In addition to the permanent exhibits, there were numerous daily events and scores of special celebrations and occasions, such as a bloodless bullfight at the Cuban Village in the Amusement Area, with Sidney Franklin as matador. There were also unlooked-for controversies, as when a number of labor unions engaged in pavilion construction and maintenance were accused of extortionate practices that dismayed some exhibitors and drove away others.

The purpose of the present book, however, is to offer not a chronicle of the transitory happenings, but an extensive record of the physical aspect of the Fair, emphasizing building exteriors and outdoor long views. It also gives a sampling of the interior exhibits and demonstrations, which made use of the latest techniques of museum curators as well as those of advertisers and industrial designers, most notably the diorama or large working model, a European development first made popular with American viewers at the 1933 Chicago fair. A number of the entertainments in the Amusement Area are also presented, but generally only those of some distinction or special interest (there is no need to show one more roller coaster, sky ride, auto dodgem, freak show, striptease act, penny arcade, shooting gallery or archery range). The individual pictures and captions included here, used in conjunction with the Index, recreate the abiding image of the Fair and catalogue some of its best-remembered artistic and scientific achievements.

The captions and Index will also indicate what

Leo Friedlander's four statues representing the *Four Freedoms* stood on Constitution Mall behind the statue of George Washington, near the Lagoon of Nations. This pre-Fair-opening shot by Richard Wurts shows a rather sulky Freedom of the Press being moved to her appointed station.

To take this picture of the Perisphere under construction, Richard Wurts had to climb straight ladders up to the very top of
the Trylon (which casts a shadow) and hang out of a trapdoor
by his legs.

a magnificent roster of varied talents was represented at this Fair: composers like Kurt Weill, Aaron Copland and Arthur Schwartz; theatrical producers and directors like Billy Rose, Mike Todd, John Murray Anderson and Margaret Webster; sculptors and painters like James Earle Fraser, Jo Davidson, Alexander Calder, Rockwell Kent and Paul Manship; the above-mentioned industrial designers N. Bel Geddes, Dreyfuss, Loewy and Teague; and architects like Alvar Aalto, Skidmore & Owings and Shreve, Lamb & Harmon. All of these were established masters displaying fresh facets of their skills and genius. But there were also younger men who would become famous at a later date: the film director Joseph Losey; the architects Morris Lapidus, Oscar Niemeyer and Sven Markelius; and a number of others.

The emphasis in this book is on the 1939 aspect of the exposition, since only in its first year did the Fair fully represent the original wishes of its planners. Well liked as it was in its initial season (ending October 31, 1939), its attendance was not nearly as great as had been hoped (nor were Manhattan shopkeepers satisfied with their profits from Fair visitors), and the financial situation of the Fair Corporation seemed to call for drastic measures.

Harvey Dow Gibson, who had been the finance chairman on the Fair's Board of Directors, became chairman of the board and business manager. (He had also had a public career, serving as American Red Cross commissioner for all of Europe in 1919.) Although Grover Whalen stayed on as president, Gibson's likeness replaced Whalen's in the 1940 edition of the *Official Guide Book* and Gibson's spirit made itself felt everywhere. The adult admission price was lowered to 50 cents. Rents to exhibitors were also reduced, and many new concessions, generally rowdier, were brought into the Amusement Area, which was renamed the Great White Way. Buildings in the main part of the grounds were reassigned in a clear bid for

broader tastes. The *Guide Book* was completely revised: all exhibits (except amusements) were listed in one alphabetical order, all division into, or reference to, zones being completely abandoned; and the style of writing was greatly popularized (compare the 1939 "In Steinmetz Hall [of the GE Building]—vivid lightning, thunderous noise, ten million volts flashing over a 30-foot arc" with the 1940 "In Steinmetz Hall, 10,000,000 volts of man-made lightning leap 30 feet through the air with a roar of thunder, scaring the daylights out of you").

Another big difference in 1940 was that the Second World War was in progress when the Fair reopened on May 11. Whalen had revisited Europe and had done wonders in keeping the foreign contingent together, but in 1940 the Soviet Union (branded as an aggressor in Finland) was gone, and Norway and Denmark were represented only by local concessions. (Argentina, Siam and the state of Georgia had also pulled up stakes.) Great Britain, Poland, Czechoslovakia and Finland had reminders of the world situation among their exhibits. The Fair Corporation smugly congratulated Americans on the country's noninvolvement in the war, and the blessings of "Peace and Freedom" replaced the "World of Tomorrow" as a watchword for the exposition.

When the Fair finally closed, on October 27, 1940, it was clear that the Corporation would have to declare bankruptcy, attendance having brought in only about 48 million dollars from about 45 million admissions, while the Corporation's expenses had exceeded 67 million. New York City forced its claims to the money it had been promised as the first slice off the receipts. Gibson attempted to interest the federal government in the grounds as a site for a military training camp, but Robert Moses saved his park. (After various protracted fiscal operations, the Corporation was dissolved in 1945.)

In the new park, the New York City Building,

intended from the start as a permanent structure, became a skating rink. After the Second World War it housed the United Nations while that organization's permanent Manhattan headquarters was under construction. In 1964/1965 another World's Fair was held in the park, with the old New York City Building and New York State Amphitheatre (it too a permanent structure) filling roles analogous to those of 1939/1940.

In 1976, Flushing Meadows Corona Park, though by no means the elegant haunt and the landscape architect's dream it had resembled in the blueprints of the mid-1930s, was a decently maintained and well-policed recreation area put to good use by local residents. A mock Revolutionary battle was enacted (not reenacted) there as part of the nation's bicentennial festivities. The New York City Building was occupied by the small Queens Museum, and the Amphitheatre was the entrance and service area of a paid bathing establishment on Meadow Lake. Assorted relics of the 1964/1965 fair included the Unisphere (where the Trylon and Perisphere had stood), the New York State Pavilion (housing the Queens Playhouse and a roller-skating rink), the United States Building (a wreck), The Singer Bowl (now Louis Armstrong Stadium), the Port Authority Heliport (not in use) and the Hall of Science (still in use in its original role). Most of the terrain that had been the Transportation area in both fairs was occupied by the Queens Zoo, where, it was repeatedly claimed, the animals were not sufficiently protected from vandalism.

As mentioned above, the present book follows the 1939 *Official Guide Book* in its observance of zones, but does not order the zones, and the buildings within the zones, in strict alphabetical order as the *Guide Book* did. Instead, the sequence of zones here is based on considerations of their intrinsic interest then and now (for instance, at the time Transportation was clearly the most popular of the zones, taking them as entities), and the sequence of buildings and sites is based on considerations of visual interest. Another departure from the 1939 *Guide Book* is the decision to be more strict here in the geographical presentation, leaving Sweden and Turkey in the Food Zone, and Florida in the Amusement Area, where they were actually located and where visitors to the Fair actually got to see them. Free-standing statues and other monuments are discussed here according to the zone in which they stood, at the end of the respective sections.

The book does not attempt to be complete; the availability of good photographs and convenience of length and format had to be taken into account. Just about all the buildings and sites that were best liked by the public and the critics, and are best remembered by old-timers, will be found here, and it is believed that a judicious cross section of the Fair has been presented. The omission of any company or organization's exhibit in no way constitutes a negative judgment as to its appearance, value or significance.

THE NEW YORK WORLD'S FAIR
1939/1940

THEME CENTER, CONSTITUTION MALL, ADMINISTRATION, GENERAL FEATURES

1. **The** Theme Center, that is, the area epitomizing the spirit and motto of the Fair, "Building the World of Tomorrow," comprised the Trylon and Perisphere and the immediately adjacent grounds. The 700-foot-high Trylon (triangular pylon) and the 200-foot-wide Perisphere, both painted pure white (outlying structures in the Theme Center were off-white), were the work of the architectural firm of Harrison & Fouilhoux (soon to participate in Hunter College and to do the African Plains at the Bronx Zoo), which submitted over a thousand sketches for this focal site of the Fair. Reproduced on thousands of different miniature souvenir items, the Trylon and Perisphere were regarded as the most imposing symbol for any fair since the Eiffel Tower of 1889. The sculpture at the right, in the Court of Power, is John Gregory's *Four Victories of Peace*, representing Wheels, Wings, Wheat and Wisdom. A hand-pushed touring chair is seen near the statue. In the foreground are some of the million tulips and other bulbs donated by Dutch growers.

2. Visitors rode part way up the Trylon on what was then the world's highest escalator, then entered the Perisphere (interior design by Henry Dreyfuss), stepping onto one of two moving rings, from which they viewed the vast diorama of Democracity, a planned urban and exurban complex of the future. The accompanying musical score by William Grant Still was conducted by André Kostelanetz and the narration spoken by the popular newscaster H. V. Kaltenborn. At the end of the six-minute show, film projections presented several groups of happy farmers and workers. Afterwards, the visitors walked back to ground level via a ramp called the Helicline.

3. One of the statues near the Perisphere was *The Astronomer* by Carl Milles, a Swede who had come to the United States in 1929 and whose civic sculpture in and around Chicago had received great acclaim. At night the Theme Center was flood-lighted, and cloud patterns were projected onto the Perisphere.

4. The Trylon and Perisphere rested on a thousand piles driven through the soft fill deep into solid ground. A walk around them at ground level yielded innumerable views of subtle geometric elegance, reminiscent of William Cameron Menzies' breathtaking sets in the 1936 science-fiction film *Things to Come*.

5. Near the Theme Center stood this sculptural sundial, called *Time and the Fates of Man*, by Paul Manship, famous for his Rockefeller Center *Prometheus* and other New York City civic sculptures. The middle ground of this photo shows crowds moving from the Trylon into the Perisphere; in two remoter planes, visitors can be seen using the Helicline to descend. Toward the lower right is a Greyhound tractor train, or lounge car, one of the means of getting around the Fair.

6 & 7. In the basin on Constitution Mall (northeast of the Theme Center), near the giant statue of George Washington, were the four *Moods of Time*, also by Manship. The female figure shaded by owls represented Night; the man awakened by the crowing cock represented Morning. Behind the small trumpeting figure can be seen the Medicine and Public Health Building, with the mural shown in No. 89.

8. All four *Moods of Time* (Night and Morning are at the extreme left and right, respectively; the others are Day and Evening) are seen in the Constitution Mall basin in front of Washington Square, site of the statue of Washington as he looked at his 1789 inauguration in New York (the Fair ostensibly commemorated the 150th anniversary of this event). The sculptor was James Earle Fraser, most famous for his design of the Indian-head nickel. Closing the vista is the United States (Federal) Building.

9. A closer view of the statue. At the left are the pylons of the Gas Industries Building in the Community Interests Zone of the Fair.

10. The large Administration Building was tucked into the farthest southwest corner of the Fair grounds across Grand Central Parkway from the Transportation Zone. Here it is viewed from the south, with its restaurant prominently facing the observer. On its eastern end it was flanked by the Fair's Post Office and the Press Building.

11 & 12. Two views, one head-on, the other a lengthwise detail, of the covered bridge connecting the Administration Building with the Press Building. A bus route ran below this bridge, which was designed by Michael L. Radoslovich and Arthur Barzagli of the Fair Corporation Design Board.

13. One of the numerous one-of-a-kind light standards scattered over the Fair grounds. It was at the 1939 fairs in New York and San Francisco (Golden Gate Exposition) that soft, cold white light—from fluorescent tubes—was first introduced to the public on a large scale. In the background is the Trylon, still unfinished when this picture was taken.

14. The chrome and neon finial of one of the seventeen Fair information booths. This one was in the Communications Zone.

15. An imposing row of fluorescent standards in the Court of Power at night. At the right is the Perisphere. A similar row of lights—the same one or its facing counterpart—can be seen at the lower left of No. 1.

16. One of several Fair fountains called Aqualons. The upright
glass tube contained moving water and goldfish.

TRANSPORTATION

17. In this overall view of the Transportation Zone, the enormous Railroads Building is at the upper left. Below it (and slightly to the right in the picture) is the Chrysler Motors Building, and below that the dome of the Aviation Building. At the lower right is the Firestone Building. Above and left is the Ford Building, then the intricate General Motors complex and finally the Goodrich Building. Across the multilaned Grand Central Parkway, the long, low, colonnaded structure is the New York City Building (still standing), with the interconnected Business Machines and Insurance Building and Business Systems Building above and to the left. At the far right, beyond the New York City Building, is the Perisphere.

18. The main entrance of the General Motors complex (architect: Albert Kahn), actually four interconnected buildings. The exhibit, known collectively as "Highways and Horizons," was the largest presented by any individual participant in the Fair. The designer was Norman Bel Geddes. There were numerous displays of new Chevrolets, Pontiacs, Oldsmobiles, Buicks, Cadillacs and La Salles (there was even a transparent acetate car), as well as Frigidaires and a Diesel-electric locomotive. A Previews of Progress science show was also offered, and there was an impressive lifesize multilevel futuristic "street intersection of 1960."

19. But the hit of General Motors and of the Fair as a whole was the Futurama ride. In this view, the main GM entrance is at the lower right, but the enormous waiting line leads to the Futurama entrance in the lower center. Inside views of this attraction appear on the next page. This picture shows clearly the "street intersection" where the four elements of the GM complex come together in the middle. Across Grand Central Parkway is the New York City Building.

20. Six hundred chairs with individual loudspeakers moved visitors over a 36,000-square-foot scale model of the highway world of 1960: seven-lane roads with permissible 100-mph speed, experimental homes, farms and urban developments, industrial plants, dams, bridges and all the intervening landscape.

21. Springing up around a planned traffic system—still looked on in 1939 as the guarantee of future happiness—the metropolis of 1960 was seen to be free of slums and blight, full of parks and civic centers. Energy sources would apparently be abundant, climate perfect. In 1964 GM offered an analogous ride at almost the same location.

22. One of the wing-like pylons of the Chrysler Motors Building (architect: James Gambrel Rogers) before the final application of paint (see No. 17). This building housed in its rotunda the Focal Exhibit of the Transportation Zone (designed by Raymond Loewy): a filmed history of transportation projected onto a vast map of the world, and a Rocketport display with a gun shooting off a shipload of passengers for London. The main part of the building was an imaginative showcase for Plymouths, Dodges, DeSotos and Chryslers, but also contained a small theater which gave the first public showing of animated color 3-D movies (about the parts of a car) with the audience using Polaroid glasses.

23. The "Ford Exposition" (architect: Albert Kahn, Inc.; designer: Walter Dorwin Teague) had a facade dominated by a free-floating stainless-steel sculpture in the round, *Mercury* by Robert Foster.

24. This aerial study of the Ford Motor Company's building shows its most notable feature at the lower left corner: the winding half-mile Road of Tomorrow over which visitors, riding in sample cars, were afforded shifting views of the Fair grounds. Just above and to the right is the Garden Court, in which the composer and arranger Ferde Grofé led a group of musicians performing on Novachords, which were Hammond keyboard instruments that simulated orchestral timbres.

25. Inside the Ford Building, apart from the expected display of Fords, Mercurys and Lincoln-Zephyrs, the main features were a vast activated mural by Henry Billings and—thought by some critics to be the most remarkable exhibit at the Fair— the 100-foot-wide revolving turntable seen at the far left in this picture, the Ford Cycle of Production, which bore 87 animated groups showing every step in the manufacture of a car, beginning with the extraction of the necessary ores.

26. In the Ford Garden Court, with the Road of Tomorrow as a stirring backdrop, stood the *Chassis Fountain* by the noted sculptor Isamu Noguchi (later work of his in New York included the Chase Manhattan Plaza fountain, the 666 Fifth Avenue waterfall and New School courtyard sculptures).

27. A large part of the Railroads exhibit, in which the 27 Eastern railroads participated, was displayed outdoors. In a vast yard were assembled numerous historic English and American locomotives, such as the famous *General* (1853) and the *Ross Winans* (1845). Here a photographer is taking a head-on close-up of the 1844 American *Daniel Nason*, which ran between Boston and Providence.

28. One of the highlights of the outdoors display was this 140-foot, 526-ton steam locomotive, the 6100, the largest ever built by the Pennsylvania's shops in Altoona. Designed by Raymond Loewy, it ran continuously at the Fair at 60 mph on a roller bed.

29. The famous Wedding of the Rails at Promontory Point, Utah, in 1869 was one of the many historical railroading events reenacted in the chief entertainment feature of the Railroads exhibit, the show *Railroads on Parade*, written, produced and directed by Edward Hungerford, who had staged railroad pageants at three previous smaller fairs. The composer of the musical score, Kurt Weill, and several other members of the technical staff had been associated shortly before in Max Reinhardt's New York production of *The Eternal Road* by Franz Werfel.

30. Inside the Railroads Building, the largest at the Fair (architects: Eggers & Higgins; consulting designer: Raymond Loewy) were various models and dioramas, the chief of which is shown here: *Railroads at Work*, designed by Paul Penhune. Housed in a thousand-seat auditorium, this 160 by 40-foot diorama included 500 pieces of equipment and demonstrated every function of railroading in a 40-minute show.

31. The 90-foot tower of the B. F. Goodrich Company Building (architects and designers: William Berl Thompson and Wilbur Watson & Associates) housed a giant "tire guillotine," with a falling and rebounding blade, that duplicated one of the company's testing devices in Akron. Outdoors, tires were tested in difficult performance conditions, and stunt drivers gave daredevil shows six times a day.

32. The Firestone Tire & Rubber Company Building (architects: Wilbur Watson & Associates; designer: George W. McLaughlin) included a small tire factory, dioramas of the company's rubber plantations in Liberia, and a full-scale model farm in which pneumatic tires were applied to everything possible.

33. Visible at the left is one of the twin prows on the facade of the Marine Transportation Building (architects: Ely Jacques Kahn and Muschenheim & Brounn). On the wall surface to the right of the prow is seen a mural by Lyonel Feininger. Inside were exhibits of navigational instruments and American steamship trade routes. In 1940 these exhibits were moved to the Communications Building, and the structure seen here became Fair Operations Building Z-1.

34. Likened by some to a blimp nosing into a band concert shell, the emblematic Aviation Building reminded its architects (William Lescaze and J. Gordon Carr) of a hangar embodying "flight in space." The exhibits were presided over by Captain Eddie Rickenbacker. The half-dome, which was entirely separate from the long hangar section, with light and air admitted between, served as a cyclorama against which suspended aircraft were dramatically displayed. This photograph, taken in 1938, shows the construction work still in progress.

35. Near the Corona Gate South in the Transportation Zone stood Benjamin Hawkins' *Samson and the Lion*, known more familiarly as "Man with a Dog by the Tail."

36. Archetypical of 1930s streamlining was this stainless-steel windsock in the area of the Budd Manufacturing Company, producers of lightweight transport units.

37. This stainless-steel fountain was also in the Budd area.

COMMUNICATIONS AND BUSINESS SYSTEMS

38. Below the Theme Center is the double structure of Business Systems and (with the rounded end) Business Machines and Insurance, in which IBM showed modern paintings from 79 countries. To the left, with protruding wings, is the Masterpieces of Art Building, which housed a priceless international loan show of paintings. The dark-roofed complex to the left of that is the Administration-cum-Press-cum-Post Office group. The long light building extending above that is the Communications Building, at the left end of which is the Star Pylon and at the right end of which are seen the tall twin pylons that stood in the Court of Communications. Just to the right of and below them is the relatively small Crosley Radio Corporation Building. Cut into by those pylons (in the photo) is the American Telephone & Telegraph Building, and to the upper left of that, on the axis that bisects the Communications Building, is the smaller RCA Building. Various other Fair zones are also seen.

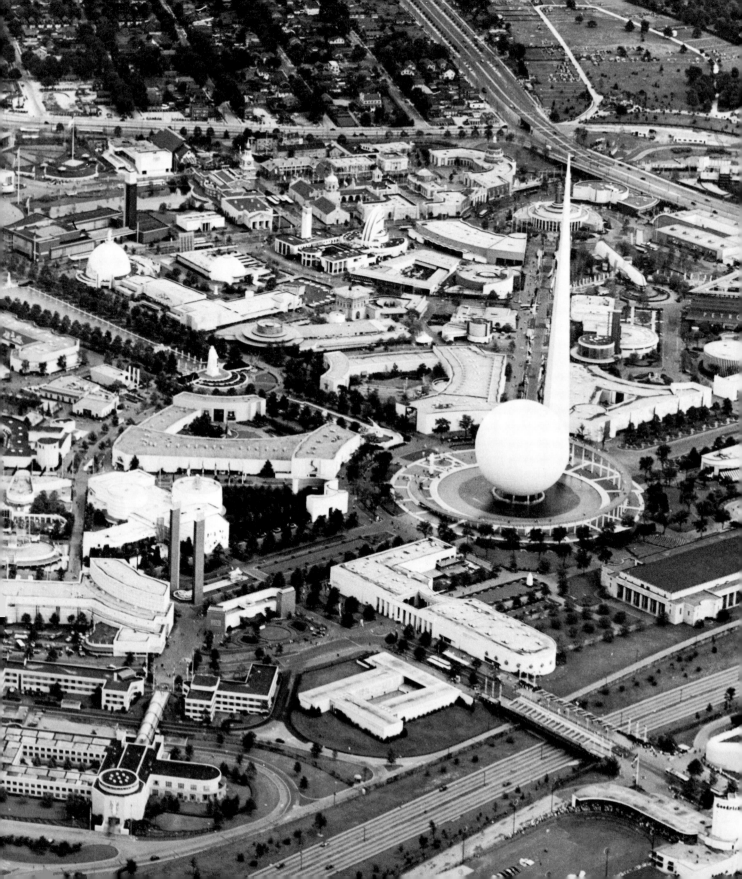

39. In front of the AT&T Building (architects: Voorhees, Walker, Foley & Smith) stood the sculptural group *The Pony Express* by Carl Milles. Exhibits inside included Pedro the Voder (Voice Operation Demonstrator), which produced synthetic English-language speech using 50 phonemes. In 1940 it sang, too.

40. Another feature of the AT&T interior (designed by Henry Dreyfuss) was the Demonstration Call Room, in which visitors chosen by lot could make a free call to anywhere in the United States.

41. Another emblematic structure, the Radio Corporation of America Building was shaped (as seen from aloft) like a radio tube. The architects and designers were Skidmore & Owings.

42. The main RCA lobby was brightened by one of the few glass curtain walls found outside of the foreign pavilions (most of the commercial pavilions eschewed windows).

43. The most unusual RCA feature was television. The sets of the time sold for several hundred dollars. In this, the finest model, the image was seen reflected in a mirror in the lid. Public telecasting in the New York City area began on the same day as the Fair. Regular programming, which included live drama, consisted of two hour-long programs per week, but special events were also covered.

44. The Star Pylon, by Francis Keally and Leonard Dean, was one of the towering landmarks of the Fair; it represented the force of electricity. The same architects were responsible for the Communications Building, in which the Focal Exhibit of this zone was located.

45

PRODUCTION
AND DISTRIBUTION

45. The industries represented in this zone were those that transform natural resources into necessary commodities and services. A flight formation of planes is seen here over the New York City Building. Below the Theme Center is the double complex of the Hall of Pharmacy (with a wing jutting toward the Perisphere) and Perylon Hall. Below, to the left, is the Electrical Products Building (with the pylon seen in No. 46). To the right of that is the Electric Utilities Exhibit (with its waterfall wall). Below, with the spiral tower, is the Westinghouse Electric Building. At the right end of the same curved ground plot is the Operations Building of the zone. Directly above that is the General Electric Company Building, flanked on the right by the hemispherical United States Steel Corporation Building. Above that is the triangular Petroleum Industry Exhibition. To the left of Petroleum, with the curved "water ballet," is the Consolidated Edison Company Building, directly above which is Glass, Incorporated. To the left, somewhat A-shaped, is the Metals Building (in 1940, the Hall of Industry), and above that, directly right of the Theme Center, is the Consumers Building, which housed the Focal Exhibit of the zone (in 1940 this building became the World of Fashion).

46. The main entrance of the Electrical Products Building (architects: A. Stewart Walker and Leon N. Gillette) was dominated by this French-blue pylon. The chief exhibitor in the building was Remington Rand, displaying electric razors, typewriters and other business machines and supplies. In the background of the picture is the unfinished Trylon. In 1940, this building was called the Power—Electrical & Steam Building, and Remington Rand had vacated.

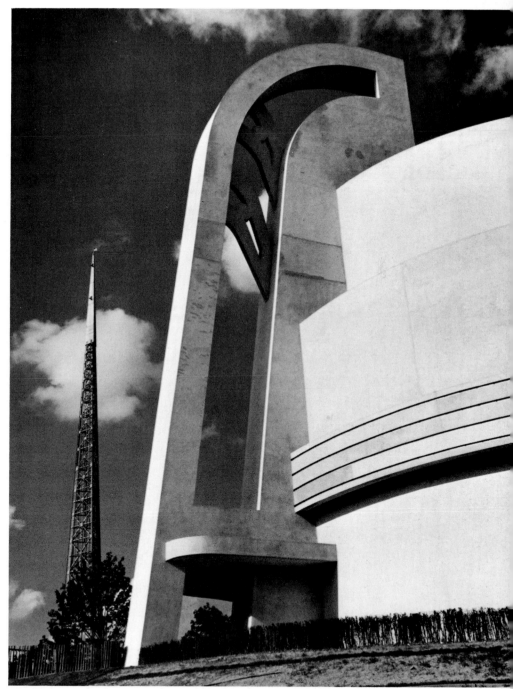

47. Harrison & Fouilhoux were the architects of this building of the Consolidated Edison Company of New York, Inc., and Affiliated Companies. The constantly changing fountain dis-play, or Water Ballet, was designed by the sculptor and illustrator Alexander Calder. It was floodlighted at night.

48. The major exhibit inside the Con Ed Building was the City of Light, designed by Walter Dorwin Teague and Frank J. Roorda. It was "the world's largest diorama," a city-block-long, three-story-high, colored, lighted and animated model of the New York metropolitan area. There were moving subways and elevators and busy factories. A full city day passed by in 12 minutes, climaxed by a sky-darkening thunderstorm.

49

49. The blue stainless-steel building of United States Steel Subsidiaries (architects: York & Sawyer; designers: Walter Dorwin Teague and G. F. Harrell) was described as being "inside out" because its structural elements were exposed. It was a hemispherical shell hung from five intersecting open-web arches with elaborate treillage. Exhibits inside dramatized steel production. The firm of York & Sawyer had done the central portion of the New-York Historical Society building in 1908, the Flower & Fifth Avenue Hospitals in 1921, the Bowery Savings Bank in 1923, and a number of other important banks.

50. The 105-foot tower of the E. I. du Pont de Nemours & Company, Inc., Building represented chemical laboratory apparatus (designers: Walter Dorwin Teague, Robert J. Harper and A. M. Erickson). The 70-foot-high steel framework around the tower symbolized the workways found in chemical plants. The most significant exhibit inside showed the spinning of nylon yarn. Already used for sutures, toothbrushes and fishing lines, nylon was here first publicized as a textile.

51. A detail of the Operations Building (designed by
Harvey Wiley Corbett/Robert W. Cutler) at night.
The murals were by Herman Van Cott.

52. The building of Glass, Incorporated, at night. The architects were Shreve, Lamb & Harmon, who did the Empire State Building (completed 1931). The tower was of plate glass and glass brick. The cooperating exhibitors were the Corning Glass Works (with Steuben glass), the Owens-Illinois Glass Company (with Libbey tableware) and the Pittsburgh Plate Glass Company.

53. The exhibits inside the Glass Building were designed by Skidmore & Owings and John Moss. Chief among them was this furnace of molten glass and glassblowers at work. Glassblowing had been a popular attraction as far back as the Chicago fair of 1893.

54. One of the most unforgettable images bequeathed by the Fair, this photograph is here printed upside down. It corresponds to No. 53 in subject matter, but it is a shot of the mirrored ceiling (world's largest) over the glassblowing display.

55. The Eastman Kodak Company Building (architect: Eugene Gerbereux; designers: Walter Dorwin Teague and Stowe Myers) featured mammoth color reproductions inside and out, and a Photo-Garden that offered unusual settings for souvenir snapshots.

56. One wall of the Electric Utilities Exhibit, in which 175 companies participated (architects: Harrison & Fouilhoux), was occupied by a waterfall and spillway. Inside, a street of 1892 (with a living cast) was contrasted with a modern street to demonstrate the blessings of electricity. At the right in the photo is seen one of the pylons shown more clearly in No. 63.

57. The stainless-steel spire of the General Electric Company Building (architects: Voorhees, Walker, Foley & Smith) symbolized the taming of electricity. The most dazzling feature inside was a ten-million-volt flash generated over a 30-foot arc. In addition, visitors were treated to an X-ray of a swathed and cased Egyptian mummy. GE products displayed inside included television.

58. One of the outstanding paintings done for the Fair was also in the GE Building: a mural designed by Rockwell Kent and painted under his direction. It represented the progress from obscurantism to enlightenment made possible by electrical research. The figure below the left tube of the generator (at the right in the mural), with left arm slightly extended above the waist, is a stylized self-portrait of the artist.

59. Published here for the first time is Kent's original drawing for the GE mural, squared off for enlargement, found among his papers in 1976. A comparison between this and the finished mural is of interest.

60. The Time Capsule, a torpedo-shaped container "bearing the message of present-day America to the people of Earth of 6939 A.D.," was buried 50 feet deep in the Immortal Well in front of the Westinghouse Electric & Manufacturing Company Building (architects: Skidmore & Owings and John Moss). The capsule held various objects and millions of pages on microfilm. An analogous capsule was buried by Westinghouse at the 1964 New York fair only a few yards away from the earlier one.

61. Also in the Westinghouse forecourt stood the Singing Tower of Light, symbol of electric power. The most popular feature inside the Ω-shaped building was Elektro, a seven-foot-tall robot that performed in numerous ways.

62. One of the structures that received most praise from quali-
fied critics was the triangular Petroleum Industry Exhibition
(architects: Voorhees, Walker, Foley & Smith). It rested on
four oil tanks and rose in flaring tiers. An active derrick was
reflected in a pool outside. Inside, you could watch a puppet
film, *Pete-Roleum and His Cousins*, directed by the 30-year-old
Joseph Losey, whose career was just shifting from stage to
screen via short subjects for advertising.

63. Separating the Court of Power from the Plaza of Light (Con
Ed's Water Ballet is seen in the background) were four 65-foot
pylons representing the four traditional elements. They featured 48 relief sculptures by Carl Paul Jennewein, a noted
artist who was still receiving imposing civic commissions in
the 1970s.

64. One of the most distinguished sculptors represented at the Fair was Jo Davidson, whose bronze portrait of Walt Whitman, called *The Open Road* or *Afoot and Light-Hearted*, stood in Perylon Court or Circle (the circular area just below the Theme Center in No. 45).

65. In the very center of Perylon Circle was Malvina Hoffman's *Dances of the Races*.

66. A portion of the Production and Distribution Zone not included in No. 45 is seen in this apocalyptic night view. In the left foreground is a corner of the du Pont de Nemours Building, and to the right of that is the "igloo" of the Carrier Corporation (architects: Reinhard & Hofmeister, among the major architects of Rockefeller Center from 1931 to 1940). Next to the right is the Elgin National Watch Company Building. Spanning it in the photo is the Empire State Bridge, leading to the Amusement Area, where the *Aquacade* was featured at the New York State Amphitheatre and (at the moment) Michael Todd's *Hot Mikado* at the World's Fair Hall of Music. The nightly firework display over the lake is in progress.

65

FOOD ZONE

67. The Focal Exhibit of the Food Zone was located in the Food Building South, or No. 3 (architects: Philip L. Goodwin —who also did the Museum of Modern Art in 1939—Eric Kebbon, Edward D. Stone, Morris Ketchum, Jr., and Richard Boring Snow). This structure, which became the Coca-Cola Building in 1940, was distinguished by its four golden wheat stalks and its long mural wall painted by Witold Gordon. The Trylon rises above the wall. Means of transportation shown are two hand-pushed chairs and one of Greyhound's tractor trains.

68. The Schaefer Center (architect: Eggers & Higgins) was a restaurant seating 1600, and had a long open-air bar.

69. A decided hit of the Food Zone was the Borden Company Building (architects and designers: Voorhees, Walker, Foley & Smith), in which 150 pedigreed cows were washed, dried and mechanically milked on a revolving platform called the Rotolactor. Other exhibits included a processing room in which the milk was pasteurized and bottled.

NATALIE OF PENN VILLA
GUERNSEY—AGE: 5
OWNER: H. B. PENNEY
Granville, Ohio

70. Some of the cows on loan from five breed associations to
Borden's "Dairy World of Tomorrow."

71. The Continental Baking Company Building (architects: Skidmore & Owings and John Moss) was dotted with red, blue and yellow balloons like those on the wrapper of Wonder Bread. Inside, you could watch this bread and Hostess Cake being baked. In the rear was the only wheatfield that had been grown in New York City for well over half a century. In the background of this pre-opening photo can be seen the top of the U.S.S.R. Pavilion with the scaffolding still around it.

72. The building of the Distilled Spirits Exhibit, Incorporated, in which 22 firms cooperated (architect: Morris Sanders; designers: Ross-Frankel, Inc., and Morris Lapidus), was outstanding for its 50-foot-high "structural banner." The displays emphasized the contributions of the liquor industry to government revenue and such related industries as farming and transport. This exhibit was not resumed in 1940. To the left in the photo is a corner of the four-part building of Standard Brands, Incorporated (Fleischmann's Yeast, Chase & Sanborn Coffee, Royal Desserts and the Baking Industry). Morris Lapidus is now better known as the architect of the Fontainebleau Hotel in Miami Beach (1954), the Miami-style Americana Hotel in New York (1962) and important housing projects and shopping centers.

73. The Beech-Nut Packing Company Building (architect and designer: Magill Smith) featured a miniaturized circus (see the mural in the entranceway) and various dioramas about the raw materials and preparation of strained foods and chewing gum.

74. The National Dairy Products Corporation (Sealtest) Building (architect: De Witt Clinton Pond) displayed the manufacture and packaging of milk, ice cream and "Philadelphia" brand cream cheese.

75. The General Cigar Company Building (architect: Ely Jacques Kahn) showed how White Owls were made. World news flashed on a screen, and automatic score boards reported major-league baseball games inning by inning. In 1940 this was called the White Owl Building.

76. The American Tobacco Company Building (architects and designers: Francisco & Jacobus) was devoted to the manufacture of Lucky Strikes.

77. Two foreign pavilions found their way into the Food Zone. The Turkish Pavilion (architects: Sidad H. Eldem and Sedat Zinciskiran) blended traditional and modern features. The tiled fountain patio seen here certainly had an Arabian Nights flavor.

78. A broadside view of the Turkish Pavilion. Exhibits inside stressed the rise of modern Turkey under Kemal Atatürk, but also included a reproduction of the great Bazaar of Istanbul and a selection of original art objects going back to the Hittite period.

79. Architectural critics extolled the Swedish Pavilion, also in the Food Zone (architect: Sven Markelius, who later participated in the New York headquarters of the United Nations), as the most civilized and appealing area at the Fair. Single-story porticoed loggias enclosed a garden courtyard. Inside, modern furniture and applied arts were displayed. The Three Crowns restaurant featured a smörgåsbord that revolved by electricity, being constantly refilled behind a partition.

80. In the Swedish courtyard were a terrace bar and this elegant glass fountain.

81. Outside the Academy of Sports (also in the Food Zone), where informal classes were given by such eminent athletes as Babe Ruth, Lou Gehrig, Gene Tunney and Jack Dempsey, stood this statue by Leo Lentilli called *Golden Sprays*, representing ideal American young womanhood.

COMMUNITY INTERESTS

82. The building toward the lower left (circular with a long curved spur) is the Home Building Center. Just below it four pylons mark the end of the long overpass leading from the IRT and BMT subway stations and opening out onto the square known as Bowling Green. The building below that, with the two "hairpins" at the corner, is the Hall of Special Events (designated at an early stage of the Fair as the Textiles Building or Hall of Fashion; in 1940 it became Fair Operations Building L-1). Above and to the right is the circular Johns-Manville Building, to the right of which is the narrow, curved American Radiator Building, and above which is the large Home Furnishings Building. Above and to the right of that will be found the Gas Exhibits (with four pylons forming a cross). The dark-roofed, horseshoe-shaped structure to the right of that (at the picture edge) is the WPA Building. To the left of the Home Furnishings Building is the Contemporary Art Building (with a jagged facade and two globular ends), above which is the Electrified Farm, and to the left of which is the far-flung Town of Tomorrow. The planted area across the river from that is Gardens on Parade. The photo also shows parts of the Food Zone and of the Government Zone clustering around the Lagoon of Nations.

83. At the other end of the Hall of Special Events (cut off by the picture edge in No. 82) was the Fair entrance from the Long Island Rail Road station, seen here. The two statues, *Industry* and *Agriculture*, were by Mahonri M. Young. Both motorized and hand-pushed touring chairs are shown in this shot.

84. The Long Island Rail Road station at the Fair was designed by Fair Corporation Design Board architect Michael L. Radoslovich.

85. The Home Furnishings Building (architect: Dwight James Baum) housed exhibits by such firms as Fuller Brush, Hoover and United States Rubber. It was also the location of the Focal Exhibit of the Community Interests Zone (designer: Gilbert Rohde). The statue seen outside the building is *American Womanhood* by Gaetano Cecere.

86. The keynote of the Community Interests Focal Exhibit was the contrast between 1789, when toil claimed 16 hours of the day, and 1939, by which, thanks to the intervening Science and Invention, this figure was cut in half. Unfortunately, no progress has been made since. In 1940 the building became "America at Home" and contained model rooms by various designers.

87. A rather somber pre-Fair-opening shot of the 90-foot pylons of Gas Exhibits, Incorporated (architects and designers: Skidmore & Owings and John Moss). At night blue and yellow gas flames shot into the sky from these towers. The joint exhibits of most of the gas utility companies of the United States and Canada—as well as 22 American gas-appliance manufacturers —included an all-gas home. The famous restaurateur George Rector gave daily lectures and demonstrations in this building.

88. Strictly speaking, the enormous double complex of the

Medicine and Public Health Building and the Science and Education Building formed two separate Fair zones with no extension beyond themselves, but the complex was located in the Community Interests area and was certainly related to it. The Medicine and Public Health Building (architects: Mayers, Murray & Phillip) had three relief sculptures by Edmond Amateis on its main facade: (left to right) *Humility* (the Devil chastising the Texan braggart Strap Buckner), *Efficiency* (Paul Bunyan) and *Benevolence* (Johnny Appleseed).

89. The Medicine and Public Health Building also boasted several murals by Hildreth Meière, best remembered for her colored low-relief plaques on the Radio City Music Hall. The mural shown here was called *The School and the Family*.

90. Inside the Medicine and Public Health Building were the Hall of Medical Science, in which the exhibits dealt with the latest methods of preventing and curing diseases, and the Hall of Man, the Focal Exhibit, which contained a transparent man, several translucent men and many gargantuan models of organs like the ear shown here. The main attraction in the Science and Education Building was the film *The City*, now considered a classic documentary (photographed and directed by Ralph Steiner and Willard Van Dyke; original outline by Pare Lorentz; narration written by Lewis Mumford and spoken by Morris Carnovsky; musical score by Aaron Copland).

91. The American Radiator & Standard Sanitary Corporation Building (architects: Voorhees, Walker, Foley & Smith) had a classical Ionic colonnade with a difference: the columns were made up of standard three-foot sections of flue lining, with copper pipe coils for volutes. Pipe fittings, valves and radiators were the components of the decorative grillework. In good weather the curtains between the columns were drawn. Heating units, air conditioners and plumbing were displayed inside.

92. The Town of Tomorrow consisted of 15 model homes suited to Atlantic Coast climatic conditions. The range of cost for construction and equipment was between $3,000 and $35,000. In each house one room was devoted to a display of the "hidden" materials used in building it. Shown here is the Bride's Home (architects: Landefeld & Hatch). This was intended for low maintenance costs, with white asbestos-cement sides, glass brick, reddish-black brick and black joints. The walls and ceilings were of grained redwood, the fireplaces of black brick. Other structures in the Town of Tomorrow were a plywood house, a glass house, a celotex house and a Motor Home, with its main entrance leading through the garage.

93. The Electrified Farm (architects: Harrison & Fouilhoux) had cattle, horses and chickens, a greenhouse, hotbeds, orchard and pasture. Over a hundred applications of electricity were demonstrated.

94. The Johns-Manville Sales Corporation Building (architects: Shreve, Lamb & Harmon) was chiefly dedicated to the wonders of asbestos, and showed hundreds of home-building materials and industrial products developed from that mineral and others.

95. The redwood-faced Contemporary Art Building (architects: Frederick L. Ackerman, Joshua D. Lowenfish and John V. Van Pelt) was called American Art Today in the 1940 renewal of the Fair. Each of the 800 works of art shown was passed by one of numerous regional committees all over the country. The exhibition was directed by Holger Cahill, at the time the National Director of the Federal Art Project. The Central Artists' Committee was comprised of Stuart Davis, Jonas Lie and Eugene Speicher for painting; John Gregory, Paul Manship and William Zorach for sculpture; and John Taylor Arms, Anne Goldthwaite and Hugo Gellert for graphics.

96. An outdoor show at the Contemporary Art Building in July 1939. In various studio workshops, visitors could also see artists at work. This building, as well as the Masterpieces of Art Building, were not originally planned by the Fair Corporation, but were instituted at a fairly late stage of preparations in response to public demand.

97. Outside the Contemporary Art Building stood *The Harp* (also called *Lift Every Voice*) by black sculptress Augusta Savage. The frame of the harp is the arm of God, the strings are singing people.

98. The building of the Works Progress Administration, U.S.A. (architects: Delano & Aldrich and Mr. Licht) was a tribute to the WPA, which had provided more than three million jobs during the Depression. Artisans, educators, engineers and entertainers provided performances and demonstrations in the auditorium and garden. In 1940 this was called the Federal Works Agency Building, and combined displays of the Public Works Administration, the Works Projects Administration, the U.S. Housing Authority, the Public Buildings Administration and the Public Roads Administration.

99. The building of the Young Men's Christian Association of the City of New York (architect: Dwight James Baum) had social facilities and sponsored tours and other YMCA services.

100. Outside the Hall of Special Events (at first designated as a textiles building) stood a sheet-steel figure by Robert Foster called *Textiles*. This abstract welded sculpture foretold the trend that was to follow the figurative style of most of the Fair statuary.

101. At one end of the same building rose this twin light tower.

102. In the center of Bowling Green, near the Home Furnishings Building, stood Waylande Gregory's *Fountain of the Atom* with playful ceramic "electrons."

103. South of the Spillway on the west side of the Flushing River was *The Tree of Life* by Lawrence Tenny Stevens. The central elm trunk represented a "majestic spirit" flanked by a man and woman carved in eucalyptus.

GOVERNMENT

104. Every night the Lagoon of Nations became a *son et lumière* show with fireworks, flames, colored fountains orchestrated by complex mechanisms and a musical accompaniment. In this view we are located in the main part of the Government Zone, or foreign section, of the Fair and looking across the Lagoon to the main commercial section. The circular building with the prominent mural is the Food Building North. The large building with glass sides at the right is the French Pavilion.

105. The Bridge of Flags, spanning the Flushing River, led from a point near the Town of Tomorrow over to the foreign section.

106. The United States (Federal) Building (architect and designer: Howard L. Cheney) was at the far end of the axis created by the Chrysler Building, the New York City Building, the Theme Center, Constitution Mall, the Lagoon of Nations and the Court of Peace, which was lined with the Hall of Nations group. A bust of President Franklin Delano Roosevelt stood in the rear garden court. The exhibits inside gave information about the federal government's services to the public.

107. This view shows how the Federal Building closed and completed the axial vista. Its two towers represented the legislature and the judiciary; the 13 columns between them were for the original states. The tower sculptures, by Harry Poole Camden, were *Peace* and *Common Accord Among the Nations of the World*.

108. The Court of States, in which 23 states and Puerto Rico were represented, was the only part of the Fair (not counting the Amusement Area) in which the Design Board tolerated replicas of historical architecture. Starting from the lower left in this view and moving clockwise, we see one wing of the New Jersey exhibit, then Georgia (a Tara-like building which housed the American Legion exhibit in 1940), then West Virginia. The nearer straight wing of the big complex at the head of the pool housed Maine, the nearer curved section belonged to Arizona; in the very center (with the Parachute Jump looming up behind it) is Virginia; the next curved section housed North Carolina; the last straight wing was for Puerto Rico. The two buildings seen on the right-hand long side of the pool are Ohio and Illinois.

109. A separate nearby pool grouped the New England states other than Maine. A feature of the joint display was a Yankee fishing schooner.

110. The exhibits in the Missouri Building included a pioneer's log cabin. This is an example of the untypical exhibits in the Court of States, which contrasted strongly with the prevalent Art Deco style of the Fair.

111. This partial view of the foreign section shows the British Pavilion at the left. Between two of the flags in front of it, the top of the tower of the Polish Pavilion is visible. Immediately to the right of the British Pavilion is the Italian Pavilion, with the goddess Roma on top. In the right foreground is the Australian Pavilion (in the same complex as New Zealand; architects: Stephenson & Turner), which was joined to the British Pavilion by a closed bridge at first-story level.

112. In 1940, as a reminder that there was a war on at home, the English displayed this captured German parachute, used to sow magnetic mines along the coast.

113. The British Pavilion (architects: Stanley Hall and Easton & Robertson) featured a replica of the Crown Jewels, one of the original manuscripts of the Magna Carta (from Lincoln Cathedral) and a genealogy of George Washington showing his direct descent from King John and from nine of the barons who became sureties for the execution of the Magna Carta.

114. The Italian Pavilion (architect: Michele Busiri-Vici) had
a statue of Roma on top. Down its facade cascaded a waterfall, at the foot of which was a monument to Marconi. Exhibits
inside were devoted to tourism, colonies, transportation and
industrial advances, including the manufacture of synthetic
wool fiber from cow's milk.

115. On the second floor of the Italian Pavilion was this restaurant run by the famous Italian Line, whose luxury ships represented the *ne plus ultra* of 1930s ocean travel (the S.S. *Conte
di Savoia* was the direct model for the restaurant installations).

116. Although it was at its last gasp in 1939, the League of Nations was represented at the Fair by this structure (architects: P. Y. de Reviers de Mauny, J. W. T. Van Erp and George B. Post & Sons). The circular turret symbolized unity, while the pentagonal base stood for "the five continents and the five races of mankind."

117. The pavilion of the Union of Soviet Socialist Republics (architects: Boris Iofan and Karo S. Alabian) was the tallest structure at the Fair after the Trylon.

The tower was faced with the same red Karelian marble as that used on Lenin's tomb. The 79-foot-high stainless-steel statue of a worker was dubbed "Big Joe" and "The Bronx Express Straphanger" by the working crews at the Fair. Features inside included a replica of a Moscow subway station and a huge map of the Soviet Union worked out in precious and semi-precious stones. The pavilion was razed before the 1940 reopening, and the space was used for the "American Common," an open area for occasional gatherings and celebrations.

118. The Polish Pavilion (architects: Jan Cybulski and Jan Galinowski) was noteworthy for its lacy metal tower covered with gilded plaques. Exhibits included 200 Polish inventions, fashions, and mementos of Polish cooperation with America.

119. The bronze statue outside the pavilion, by Stanislaw Kazimierz Ostrowski, represented King Wladyslaw II Jagiello, who defeated the Teutonic Knights in 1410 and founded a mighty Polish dynasty. The sculpture now stands in Central Park.

120. The Hall of Oslo in the Norwegian Pavilion (architect: Finn Bryn). The exterior made interesting use of glass and wood paneling in natural finish. In 1940, this pavilion had no exhibit, only a bar and restaurant.

121. Iceland was one of the countries that had no separate pavilion, but exhibited in the extensive Hall of Nations area bordering the Court of Peace. A statue of the Icelander Leifr Eiriksson, credited with explorations of North America about 1000 A.D., stood outside; it was a replica of a bronze statue standing in Washington, D.C.

122. Finland's exhibit in the Hall of Nations was designed by the celebrated architects Alvar Aalto and his wife Aino Marsio-Aalto, who made it largely a "Symphony in Wood," accompanied by Sibelius' music. This view shows a display of skiing equipment, axes and furniture.

123. The Romanian House (architects: Prince George Cantacuzino, Octav Doicescu and Aurel Doicescu) was built of native marble in a style reminiscent of the country's monasteries. The restaurant, of which the entrance is shown here, served such dishes as stuffed vine leaves and cornmeal mush (*mamaliga*).

124. Greece's exhibit in the Hall of Nations had outer walls of colored marble. The statue is a replica of Praxiteles' *Hermes*

with the Infant Dionysus. The quotation, adapted from Pindar's Thirteenth Olympian Ode, reads: "In the land dwell Good Government and those sisters: Justice, secure foundation of cities, and Peace, of similar habits."

125. The Portuguese Exhibit (architects: Antonio Lopez and Jorge Segurado) was largely devoted to that country's great navigators and explorers.

126. A sculptural group at the Luxembourg Exhibit (architect: J. P. Michels).

127. Part of the vast painting on glass in the reception hall of the Netherlands Exhibit (architect: Dirk Slothouwer). The arts of Java and Bali, still Dutch possessions at the time, were part of the display.

128. Lucio Costa and Oscar Niemeyer Soares (later the master builder of Brasilia) embodied the precepts of their teacher Le Corbusier in their Brazilian Pavilion, with its ramp leading to an esplanade and its *brise-soleil* louvers. In the garden were native plants. Brazilian products, especially coffee, were displayed indoors.

129. The Venezuela Building (designers: Skidmore & Owings and John Moss; art directors of exhibit: Lopez Mendez and F. J. Narvaez) had glass walls and no doors. Coffee, cocoa, oil and orchids were the nation's boast. Orchids were continually flown in and hung on sculptured trees. The "Altar of the Good Neighbor" contained a lock of Washington's hair that Lafayette had transmitted to Simon Bolivar.

130. The native-style garden (landscaping: Go Tamura) was naturally an important feature of the Japanese Pavilion. The building itself was modeled after a Shinto shrine. The teas and other products of Formosa (Taiwan), then still Japanese, were featured. What may have been the most tasteless exhibit at the Fair was a costly replica of the Liberty Bell—a silver shell studded with 11,600 cultured pearls and 400 diamonds.

131. The Canadian Pavilion (architect: F. W. Williams) would have been incomplete without totem poles and Mounties. Tourism and industry received equal shares of the exhibition space.

AMUSEMENTS

132. What is now Meadow Lake (Fountain Lake in 1939, Liberty Lake in 1940) was ringed by the Amusement Area (not officially a zone; no focal exhibit), in 1940 renamed the Great White Way. Elaborate firework displays occurred nightly. The palm tree was part of the Florida exhibit on the west side of the lake.

133. However highminded the aims of the Fair Corporation and however educational some of the Amusement Area entertainments, the timeless and universal aura of carnie and Coney were all-pervasive.

134. By far the most successful concession at the Fair (even though its separate admission prices were 40 cents and a dollar) was Billy Rose's *Aquacade*, staged by master showman John Murray Anderson, who had worked with Rose on previous water pageants. The site was the New York State Amphitheatre (architects: Sloan & Robertson), seating 10,000. The show design was by Albert Johnson, the costumes by Raoul Pene du Bois, the dance direction by Robert Alton. The music, by Dana Suesse and others (lyrics by Billy Rose and Ted Fetter), was conducted by Vincent Travers.

135. The 1939 stars, seen together here, were swimming champions Johnny Weissmuller (on loan from Tarzan movies) and Eleanor Holm (who was soon to be Mrs. Rose). Channel crosser Gertrude Ederle was also in the show. Broadway baritone (once with the Metropolitan Opera) Everett Marshall and peppy Frances Williams sang. In 1940 Vincent Lopez' orchestra appeared, and Buster Crabbe replaced Weissmuller, who was transferred to the *Aquacade* at the San Francisco Golden Gate Exposition; there his leading lady was a young girl new to show business, Esther Williams.

136. The largest revolving stage in the world was used in *American Jubilee*, a historical pageant created especially for the 1940 renewal of the Fair (conceived, produced and designed by Albert Johnson; staged by Leon Leonidoff of Radio City; dances by Catherine Littlefield of the Philadelphia Ballet; costumes by Lucinda Ballard; lyrics and dialogues by Oscar Hammerstein II; music by Arthur Schwartz; starring Lucy Monroe, Ray Middleton, Paul Haakon and Wynn Murray). A coach actually used by Washington was featured in this scene of his arrival at Federal Hall for his inauguration.

137. The Merrie England area was—and here the 1939 *Official Guide Book* must be quoted verbatim—"a faithful reproduction of an Old English Village, its exterior wall simulating the Tower of London, its main entrance resembling that of Hampton Court." Of the many diversions offered, the most cultural were abridged versions of Shakespeare, prepared and directed by Margaret Webster and costumed by David Ffolkes, who had worked with her on the major Broadway revival of *Richard II* in 1937. These short plays were given in a reconstruction of the Globe. Here is a moment from *The Taming of the Shrew*. (Not renewed in 1940.)

138. The World's Fair Hall of Music (architects: Reinhard & Hofmeister), which seated 2500, had a totally unbroken sweep of roof; there were no side walls or plane surfaces. Intended for highbrow performances (the opening concert featured Josef Hofmann and John Barbirolli), it was used very soon for long runs of brassy Michael Todd Broadway musicals in Fair versions: in 1939, *The Hot Mikado*, with Bill Robinson; in 1940, *Streets of Paris*, with Abbott and Costello and Gypsy Rose Lee.

139. Another popular attraction was the Life Savers Parachute Tower, or Parachute Jump, which continued its long career in Coney Island. This awesome ride was based on contraptions used by the military to train real parachutists.

140 & 141. Two details from the facade of Salvador Dali's Dream of Venus (or Living Pictures). The three-dimensional exhibits by the master commercializer of Surrealism included his notorious couch in the shape of Garbo's lips. (Not renewed in 1940.)

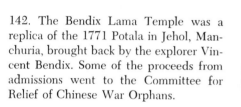

142. The Bendix Lama Temple was a replica of the 1771 Potala in Jehol, Manchuria, brought back by the explorer Vincent Bendix. Some of the proceeds from admissions went to the Committee for Relief of Chinese War Orphans.

143. A picturesque camel driver from Frank Buck's Jungleland (see also No. 150).

144. Southern Rhodesia had a standard-type exhibit in the Hall of Nations area, but its most spectacular contribution to the Fair was located in the Amusement Area: this 186-foot-long replica of Victoria Falls on the Zambezi. Native drums were heard above the roar of waters. The building that housed it (designer: Norman Yule) also contained a simulated rain forest. (Not renewed in 1940.)

145. Heineken's on the Zuider Zee was the fully descriptive
name of this tavern area.

146. Fifty independent Seminole tribesmen, who maintained their own police force and jail at the Fair, went about numerous daily activities in public at the Seminole Village. Wrestling alligators was all in the day's work. (Not renewed in 1940.)

147. Just as Turkey and Sweden ended up in the Food Zone, so Florida was wrested from its sister states and placed in the Amusement Area. But it appeared to thrive there, on a much larger tract than any other state's, with a building constructed entirely of native materials and sporting a carillon tower. At the entrance was a large talking statue of Ponce de Leon, inviting the passerby to step in.

148. The show known as the Arctic Girl's Tomb of Ice featured a classic outside come-on pitch. It was even possible to converse with the scantily clad, "self-hypnotized" girl embedded in the 1400-pound cake of clear ice. (Not renewed in 1940.)

149. A pitchman also gathered crowds outside Old New York, which was supervised by George Jessel and aimed at recalling the Gay Nineties, with Steve Brodie diving from a 100-foot-high Brooklyn Bridge. There was a "ghetto restaurant" (this still meant Jewish), a reproduction of Barnum's Museum and other nostalgic entertainments. (Not renewed in 1940.)

150. This baboon lived in Frank Buck's Jungleland, in the shadow of a miniature mountain populated by several hundred rhesus monkeys; many other animals were exhibited, including elephants and a trained orangutan. There was also an authentic replica of a Malay jungle hunting camp.

151. One of the most highly praised areas of the Fair was the six-acre Children's World, Inc., complex (architect: George Howe), which centered about this witty, stylized "Trip Around the World" traversed by Gimbel Brothers' miniature stream-lined trains, with the possibility of boat and burro excursions. Also included were R. H. Macy & Company's Toyland (a museum of toys), George Hamid's seven-act one-ring circus, a pet show, rides and a restaurant for children operated by the Borden Company.

145

INDEX

The Roman numerals refer to the pages of the Introduction. The Arabic numerals are those of the captions in the main part of the book. Only proper names are indexed.